Sharon Rosenzweig and
Present...

THE COMIC TORAH

SHARON ROSENZWEIG   AARON FREEMAN

BEN YEHUDA PRESS

FOR RUTH and JOSEPH

The Comic Torah

Published by Ben Yehuda Press

http://BenYehudaPress.com

For permission to reprint contact
Ben Yehuda Press
430 Kingston Road
Teaneck, NJ 07666
permissions@benyehudapress.com

First edition
hc ISBN 978-1-934730-53-9
pb ISBN 978-1-934730-54-6

Printed in China

ANNUALLY, Jews read all five books of Moses: Genesis, Exodus, Leviticus, Numbers and Deuteronomy. The method is to read one portion every week, though some weeks are doubled up to make everything fit. The Comic Torah depicts all fifty-four Torah portions and presents a snapshot of the arguments we had this year. Next year, different arguments!

TABLE of CONTENTS

ART THERAPY

BERESHIT – GENESIS 1:1-6:8

3

EROTIC ISSUES

DEAL MEMO

LECH LECHA GENESIS 12:1-17:27

BELIEVING She may have found a completely COMPLIANT PROGENITOR for Her ARMY of DIVINE CONQUEST, YHWH appears to Abram in a DREAM:

Abram, you will be a great nation!

Your heirs will CONQUER CANAAN. Kings will SPRING from your loins.

And all I have to do is EVERYTHING You say?

RESISTANCE is FUTILE.

Let's step OUTSIDE!

Can you count to INFINITY times LIMITLESS? THAT's how many CHILDREN you'll have.

But will they call, will they WRITE?

Your SEED will cover The Land!

I FEEL my ROYALTY RISING ALREADY!

But how will I KNOW it's MINE?

FEED ME!

THE REALLY BIG ASK

PUPPY LOVE

CHAYEI SARAH - GENESIS 23:1-25:18

KEEPING WHAT'S YOUR BROTHER'S

TOLDOT — GENESIS 25:19-28:9

GENETIC ENGINEERING

VAYEITZEI – GENESIS 28:10-32:3

FLEEING his brother, Esau, JACOB headed toward HARAN. One night, he SLEPT and DREAMED of a STAIRWAY to HEAVEN.

Good luck!

GOOD JOB!

ANGELS

YHWH

Jacob, I'll make you a GREAT NATION, your SEED plentiful as DUST—

Get me FOOD, CLOTHES, and a SAFE trip HOME. Then you can be my god.

DEAL!

Laban, I love your daughter, RACHEL. She's EASILY worth 7 years of LABOR.

But for 14 years of work, you'll get four wives, 13 kids and a WILDLY DYSFUNCTIONAL FAMILY!

DEAL!

Jacob LOVED Rachel, though she was BARREN, and he HATED Leah, whose womb was OPEN.

This caused much domestic turmoil.

MY BROTHER'S FEARER

VAYISHLACH - GEN. 32:4-36:43

17

DON'T STOP DREAMING

VAYEISHEV - GENESIS 37:1-40:23

19

DREAMS **NOT** DEFERRED

MIKEITZ - GENESIS 41:1-44:17

21

JO'S BRO SHOW

VAYIGASH - GENESIS 44:18-47:27

23

JAKE & JO NO MO

VAYECHI - GENESIS 47:28-50:26

25

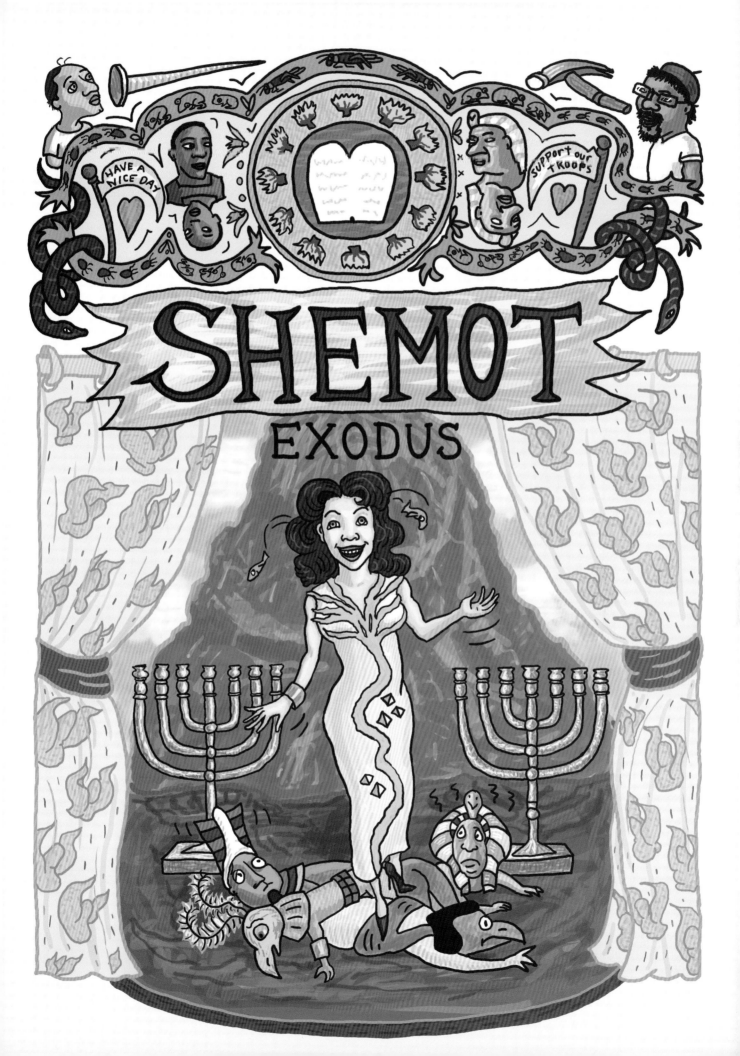

GOD OF TRICKS

SHEMOT - EXODUS 1:1-6:1

USAMA BIN YHWH?

VA'EIRA - EXODUS 6:2-9:35

33

MY BROTHER'S TRYST

MISHPATIM - EXODUS 21:1 - 24:18

YHWH'S RV

TERUMAH - EXODUS 25:1 - 27:19

YHWH'S BOY TOY

TETZAVEH - EXODUS 27:20-30:10

YHWH DON'T PLAY DAT

KI TISA - EXODUS 30:11- 34:35

YHWH passed before Moses. She covered his eyes to hide Her **FRONT**, but allowed him to glimpse Her **DIVINE BACKSIDE**.

FROM THEN ON, MOSES wore a **VEIL**, which he would **REMOVE ONLY** when he **SPOKE** with **YHWH**.

43

HOLY CONSTRUCTION CREW!

VAYAKHEL/PEKUDEI - EXODUS 35:1-40:38

VAYIKRA

LEVITICUS

MISHKAN MEALTIME

VAYIKRA – LEVITICUS 1:1-5:26

THE SACRIFICIAL CHEF

TSAV – LEVITICUS 6:1–8:36

UP IN SMOKE

SHEMINI – LEVITICUS 9:1-11:47

SKIN COLOR ISSUES

TAZRIA - LEVITICUS 12:1-13:59

53

BLOOD, BIRDS & BABES

METZORA - LEVITICUS 14:1-15:33

The METZORA (guy with white patches on his skin) has been QUARANTINED. He is now dark enough to RETURN to the camp, but first he must perform RITUAL ACTS of PENITENCE. He must—

capture two birds

Find a RED WORM...

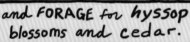

and FORAGE for hyssop blossoms and cedar.

He must then go before the HIGH PRIEST.

yit ga dal v'yit Kadesh...*

*mourner's prayer

The priest will slaughter one bird into an earthenware vessel...

Who thinks this stuff UP?

He will dip the live bird and the hyssop and the cedar in the blood of the slaughtered one...

55

GOATS & SOULS

ACHAREI MOT - LEVITICUS 16:1-18:30

A SHRILL SMALL VOICE

KEDOSHIM - LEVITICUS 19:1-20:27

59

WHAT I DID FOR LOVE

EMOR - LEVITICUS 21:1-24:23

THE PROMISED LAND

BEHAR - LEVITICUS 25:1-26:2

EXIT STRATEGY

BECHUKOTAI - LEVITICUS 26:3-27:34

65

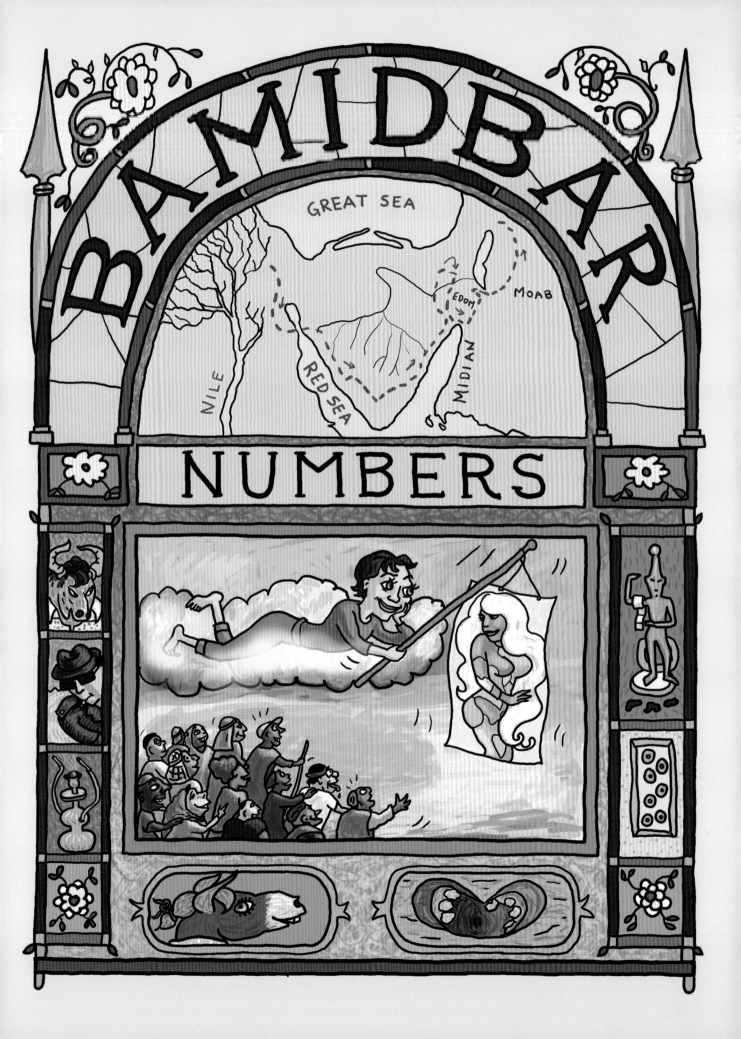

THIS MEANS WAR

BAMIDBAR - NUMBERS 1:1-4:20

Seeing beyond the Sinai, YHWH SPIES Her paramour, HONEY "The Land" Milkand, in the embrace of Her RIVAL god, MOLECH.

Moses addressed the AFL-CIO: Adonai's Federation of Levites—Congress of Idolatry Opponents.

BAD GIRLS

NASO – NUMBERS 4:21-7:89

69

YES WE CANAAN!

SHELACH - NUMBERS 13:1-15:41

KINDER, GENTLER YHWH?

KORACH - NUMBERS 16:1 - 18:32

YHWH'S ASSES

BALAK - NUMBERS 22:2-25:9

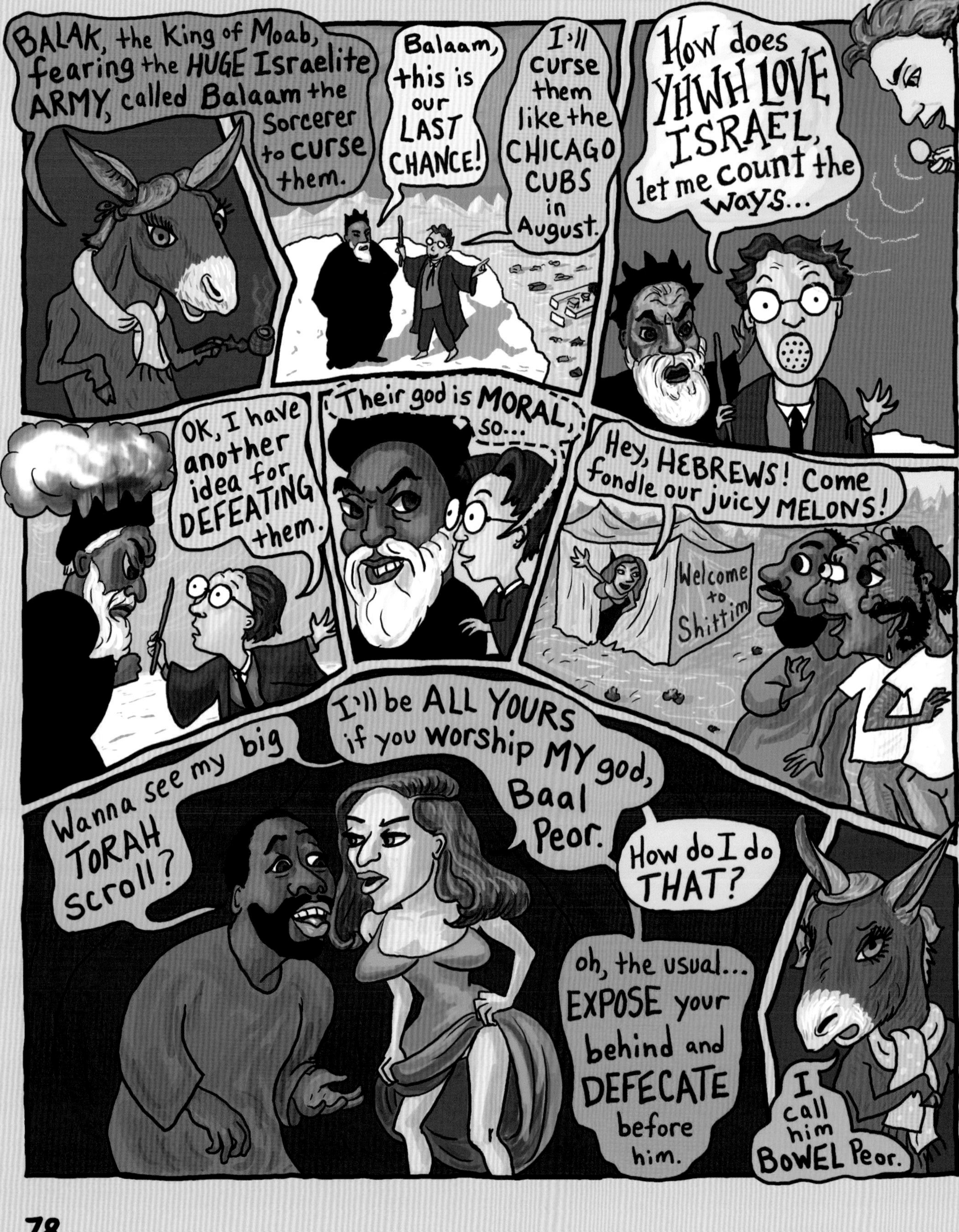

83

LAST TANGO IN SINAI

MASSEI – NUMBERS 33:1 - 36:13

SHE SAID / WE SAID

DEVARIM - DEUTERONOMY 1:1-3:22

89

91

GENOCIDE JUSTICE

SHOFTIM
DEUT. 16:18-21:9

PRETTY WOMEN

KI TEITZEI - DEUT. 21:10-25:19

When you go out to a WAR of Choice, and YHWH DELIVERS your enemies into your hands, and You see a BEAUTIFUL WOMAN among the captives and are ATTRACTED to her...

...you may TAKE her to be your WIFE and bring her to your house. There she must...

trim her hair,

cut her nails,

and discard the clothes she had when CAPTURED.

She must STAY in your house a FULL MONTH, mourning her father and mother.

MY GOD, MY BRIDE

KI TAVO - DEUTERONOMY 26:1-29:8

MO'S FINAL DAY

VAYELECH – DEUTERONOMY 31:1-31:30

103

Other Torah titles from *Ben Yehuda Press*

Torah & Company
The weekly portion of Torah,
accompanied by generous helpings
of Mishnah and Gemara, served up
with discussion questions to spice
up your Sabbath table.

Judith Z. Abrams

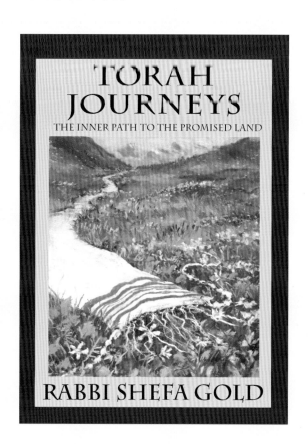

TORAH
JOURNEYS
THE INNER PATH TO THE PROMISED LAND

RABBI SHEFA GOLD

"Isidore Century is a wonderful poet. His poems are funny,
deeply observed, without pretension." – *The Jewish Week*

**from the Coffee House
of Jewish Dreamers**
poems of the weekly
Torah Portions

Isidore Century

SHMUEL KLITSNER

WRESTLING
JACOB
Deception, Identity, and Freudian Slips in Genesis

see our whole catalog at **BenYehudaPress.com**

TEAM YHWH: The BACKERS BEHIND the BOOK

Sarah Aboody

Shaun Abrahamson

Rabbi Ruth Adar

Ageless North Shore

Garrett Albright

David Aaronson

Navi Arnett

Ellie Barbarash

Nancy Barnett

Rachel Baum

Jonathan Baylis

Jeffrey Benkoe

Phyllis Benstein

Yehuda Berger

Steven Bergson

Michael Bernholtz

Ed Blachman

Bruce Bloom

Lisa Bock

Tracy Boland

Heather Booth

Jessica Borden

Patricia Brafford

Alan Brill

Paul Buch

L. Lee Butler

Bradley Caviness

John & Trish Clark

Debra Nussbaum Cohen

Margaret Cohen

Zeo Cohen

Maddy De Leon

Tom Drews

Larry Farber

Larry Feder

Rabbi Sue Fendrick

Linda Finkle

ML Frank

Sam Fried

Ellen Garvey

Val Gendleman

Robert Gluck

Rick Goheen

Jake Goodman

Ellen Gradman

Jordana Greenblatt

Beth Hamon

Karl Harkins

Diane Hoffman

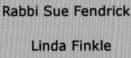

Michael Hoffman

F Penina Hoffnung

David Holzel

Jan Lisa Huttner

Shoshana Jedwab

Michelle Jones

Alexis and David Kanarek

Andrea Kantrowitz

Bluma & Stanley Kaplan

Peta Kaplan

Joel Alan Katz

Sharon Kirschner

Lyric Kite

D'vora K'lilah

Kelly Kraines

Nancy Kramer

Nancy Kullman

Jessica Leigh Lebos

Aaron Lewis

Rabbi Elias Lieberman

Suzy Lowinger

Janet Madden

Juna Berry Madrone

Dave Maleckar

Michael Maleckar

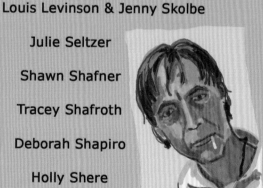

ABOUT THE CREATORS

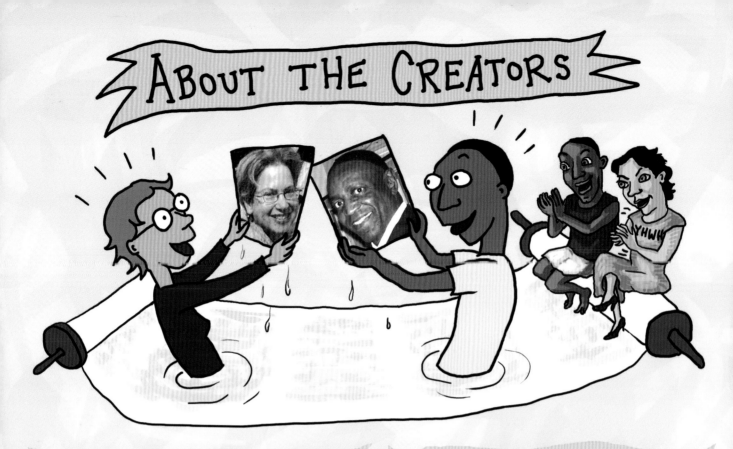

SHARON ROSENZWEIG

taught painting and printmaking at the School of the Art Institute of Chicago from 1996-2006. She has a MFA in painting from SAIC and a BFA in painting from Indiana University. She also studied at the Arts Students' League in New York.

Since 2006, Sharon has collaborated with her husband, Aaron, on cartoons, comics and Shabbat dinners. Their menus, including Sharon's famous challah, are themed to each week's Torah portion.

Previous projects include a book, *How to Say, "I Love You!" in 30 Languages*; political cartoons for The Huffington Post, and entries in the Israeli Anti-Semitic Cartoon Contest. Sharon's first cartoon was included in Art Spiegelman's article on the Mohammed cartoons in Harper's Magazine, June 2006, *Drawing Blood*.

AARON FREEMAN

is a comedian, auctioneer and MC. In his role as Torah Maven for Congregation Aitz Hayim in Highland Park, Illinois, he is the first congregational meturgeman in a thousand years of Jewish history.

Aaron is an alum of Chicago's famed Second City Comedy Troupe. He has written and starred in numerous theater hits including Council Wars, Do the White Thing, Gentlemen Prefer Bonds and The Arab-Israeli Comedy Hour.

Aaron is a member of the internationally acclaimed Israeli/Palestinian Comedy Tour, a science reporter and talk show host. Aaron's other books include, *Confessions of a Lottery Ball - The Inside Out World of Aaron Freeman*, and *Baby Boomers - From Acid Rock to Acid Reflux*.

Yippee!

...and there's MORE!! Our MODERN MIDRASH Workshop... Jewish Standup Comedy... Torah as Cook Book... VIDEO Torah... PLUS more Comics, Characters and FUN... All @ THEComicTorah.com